Presented to

_____

From

_____

Date

_____

THE PRESCHOOLERS BIBLE

Ages: 3-5

My child needs to know that God's Word
is special and life-changing.

Biblical Value: Faith

Learning Styles:

Help your child learn about God's Word in the following ways:

Sight: Each day try to read one of these Bible stories to your child. After you read, go back and look together at the pictures. Ask questions about the people, objects and events to be sure your child understands the story clearly. Point out the expressions on faces and ask how the people in the pictures might feel. Pray together afterward and thank God for His wonderful Word and the lessons it teaches us.

Sound: Read the last Bible story in *The Preschoolers Bible*, "A Boy Named Timothy." Explain that Timothy learned to love God because his mother and grandmother read God's Word to him and prayed with him. They set a good example for him, and he became a good example to others. Help your child memorize and say this Bible promise about learning and trusting God's Word: "Every word of God proves true," (Proverbs 30:5, RSV).

Touch: Help your child create "My Bible Book." Using the author's list of Bible doctrines on pages 420-425, select a lesson learned from one of the Bible stories. An example might be, "God protects us from danger." Have your child draw a picture of a real-life illustration of the lesson. Be ready to help out with ideas. Do as many as possible as you read through the stories in *The Preschoolers Bible*. In time, you will have enough to collect in a binder or staple inside a cover made of construction paper.

The PRESCHOOLERS Bible

The PRESCHOOLERS Bible

V. Gilbert Beers

Illustrated by Teresa Walsh

Equipping Kids for Life

COOK COMMUNICATIONS MINISTRIES
Colorado Springs, Colorado • Paris, Ontario
KINGSWAY COMMUNICATIONS LTD
Eastbourne, England

Discover two tools to help children
apply these Bible stories; see Bible
Doctrines and Character Values
lists starting on page 420.

Faith Kidz® is an imprint of
Cook Communications Ministries, Colorado Springs, Colorado 80918
Cook Communications, Paris, Ontario
Kingsway Communications, Eastbourne, England

The Preschoolers Bible
© 1992 by Educational Publishing Concepts, Inc., Wheaton, Illinois
Text © 1994 by Gilbert Beers

Printed in Thailand

14 15 16 17 18 19 20 Printing/Year 10 09 08 07 06

ISBN-13: 978-1-5647-6317-4
ISBN-10: 1-5647-6317-X

Contents

To Parent and Teacher

Perhaps you have a copy of *The Toddlers Bible*.
Perhaps you have read it to your child during the
vitally important toddler years. Now you are
ready to move up with your child into the
preschooler years. You want to take the next steps
in your child's walk with God.

Like *The Toddlers Bible, The Preschoolers Bible*
introduces your child to just the right amount of
Bible for that age-level. Preschoolers are not ready
yet for Amos, Obadiah, Zechariah and many
other passages of the Bible. Here is just enough to
introduce the preschooler to portions of the Bible
and help him or her begin a lifetime of Bible
learning.

The key to Bible learning is Bible delight.
Please don't force-feed your child with the Bible.
It will turn that precious heart and mind the other
way, away from the Lord. Cultivate in his or her
mind a delight in the beauties of His Word, the
joys of God speaking to us.

Like *The Toddlers Bible, The Preschoolers Bible*
is filled with delightful art. Words and phrases are

within the child's reach. Not only that, the heart of the communications process flows from the heart of an author with forty years of parenting (five children who all grew to delight in the Lord and His Word), and eleven years of grandparenting (all eight are well on their way to the delights of His Word and His Presence).

The Preschoolers Bible walks softly and lovingly through the highlights of the Word. It speaks with warmth and love, for it was born with preschoolers on my lap and in my life. But this little Bible is faithful to the key teachings of the Word. The most important doctrines of the Bible are woven gently and lovingly into the young preschool child's mind and heart. Thus Christian character is formed.

Spend some of the richest hours of your life in the joys of parenting, reading daily from this easy-to-read and easy-to-learn little Bible. Start today. You will be eternally grateful as you watch your preschooler develop a growing love and delight for the Lord and His Holy Word.

—V. Gilbert Beers

God Makes Wonderful Things

Do you see the moon in the sky? Do you see the stars? Do you see the bright light from the sun? Long ago there was no moon. There were no stars. There was no bright sun to give us light. The sky was dark and empty.

16

Do you see your family? Do you see your friends? Do you see animals and birds? Long ago there were no people. There were no animals and birds. There were no trees or flowers. There was nothing at all.

God says something wonderful. When He does, special things happen. The sun begins to shine. The moon appears and gives soft light. Stars twinkle. Birds sing sweet songs. Animals run and play.

God makes everything. He makes the sun, moon, and stars. He makes the world. He makes animals and birds. He makes flowers and trees. God makes all these beautiful things for you and me. Thank You, God, for everything.

God Makes Adam and Eve

God made beautiful things in the
skies. He made a wonderful world.
Then He filled His lovely world with
special things. Everything was bright
and beautiful.

"Who will take care of My beautiful world?" God says. Then God has a good idea. He will make a man. This man will take care of God's beautiful world.

God makes a man. He calls the man
Adam. He also makes a woman. Her
name is Eve. Adam and Eve will take
care of God's world. They will enjoy
all the beautiful things God has made.

God made other people too. He made
your parents and friends. God made
you and me. "Thank You, God, for
making my parents. Thank You, God,
for making my friends. Thank You,
God, for making me."

The Garden of Eden

God wants to give Adam and Eve a special home. So He makes a beautiful garden. He calls it Eden. Adam and Eve can live there. They have everything they need. Do you think they said, "Thank You, God"?

God put many trees in Eden. Some
have good fruit. "You may eat any of
the fruit," God says. "But you cannot
eat the fruit from THAT tree." That is
a special tree. The fruit will do special
things.

Satan comes to Eden one day. He
wants Adam and Eve to disobey God.
"The fruit on THAT tree is the best,"
he tells them. What will Adam and
Eve do? God said, "Don't eat it."
Satan said, "Eat it."

The fruit on THAT tree looks wonderful. Adam and Eve want it so much. So they eat some of the special fruit. They disobey God. "You must leave your wonderful garden," God says. Now they are sorry they have disobeyed God.

Noah Builds a Big Boat

"I will send a big flood," God tells
Noah. "It will cover all the earth. If
you do what I say, you will be safe."
Noah listens carefully. He will do
what God tells him. Noah always tries
to obey God.

"Build a big boat," God says to Noah.
God tells Noah what kind of boat to
build. He tells Noah how big the boat
should be. Noah obeys God. He
makes the big boat. He makes it the
way God says.

Noah's big boat is REALLY big. It is bigger than three houses. "Put animals on the boat," God says. He tells Noah which animals. He tells Noah how many animals. Noah does what God says. He obeys God.

Noah puts the animals on the big
boat. Then Noah puts his family on
the big boat. God tells him to do this.
Noah and his family obey God. They
do everything God says they should
do.

God Sends a Big Flood

"Go on the big boat," God tells Noah.
"Take your family on it." Noah does
what God says. Noah always obeys
God. One day it begins to rain. It rains
all day. It rains all night. It rains many
days and nights.

The rain keeps coming down. Soon
there is water everywhere. The water
is higher than the trees. Then it is
higher than the mountains. Noah is
glad now that he obeyed God.

God takes care of Noah and his family.
They have food to eat. They have water
to drink. And they are safe on the big
boat. The flood will not hurt them.
Noah is glad that he obeyed God.

"Thank You, God," Noah prays. Noah thanks God each day for taking care of him. Noah loves God. God loves Noah. Are you glad Noah obeyed God? Are you glad when you can obey God too?

The Tower of Babel

Some men are building a tall tower.
They want their tower to reach to
heaven. People will think they are
important. Some people might think
they are more important than God.

These are proud men. But God does
not like pride. Sometimes proud men
think they are like God. Sometimes
they think they are better than God.

One day God makes these men stop
building their tower. They cannot
build it anymore. God makes them
leave that place. These proud men
have to go away to many different
places.

38

The proud people are not proud now.
They do not think they are important
anymore. They know that God is more
important than any tower. Now they
know they need God.

When Isaac Is Born

Abraham loves God. God loves Abraham. Long ago God promised Abraham a son. But now Abraham is getting old. He is 100 years old. He and Sarah are too old to have a baby.

How can God keep His promise?
Abraham wonders. How can He give
me the son He promised? "I WILL
give you a son," God says. God
always keeps His promises. He will
keep His promise to Abraham.

One day Sarah and Abraham DO have
a baby. God can do anything, can't He?
He can even help old people have a
baby. That's what He did for Abraham
and Sarah.

Abraham and Sarah name their baby
Isaac. He will grow to be an important
man. God will do good things
through Isaac and his family. "Thank
You, God, for our new baby,"
Abraham and Sarah must pray often.

Esau and Jacob Are Born

Isaac and Rebekah have no children.
"Please give us a baby," they pray.
Will God do it?

Then God listens to Isaac and
Rebekah. They pray for a baby. God
answers their prayers. He gives them
TWO babies. God gives them twin
sons.

Esau will become a great hunter. He will have many children. He will be an important man. But God has special plans for Jacob. Jacob's family will be called Israelites. God will do special things through them.

Much of the Bible is about Jacob's family. Do you know about Joseph and Moses? They were part of Jacob's family. So were Joshua and Gideon and King David. Jacob was an important little baby, wasn't he?

Esau Sells His Birthright

Jacob and Esau are twin brothers.
Esau likes to hunt. Jacob likes to stay
home and help his parents. Their
father likes Esau the hunter better.
Their mother likes Jacob the helper
better.

One day Esau goes hunting. Jacob
stays home to make some stew. He
cooks a big pot of stew. When Esau
comes home he is hungry. He has
hunted all day. But he has found
nothing.

"Give me some of your stew," Esau asks Jacob. "I will trade my stew for your birthright," says Jacob. Esau is a little older than Jacob. He has the birthright. Someday he will lead their tribe.

But Esau is hungry. So he trades his birthright for a pot of stew. Esau gets Jacob's stew. Jacob gets Esau's birthright. What do you think of these two brothers?

Isaac Does Not Fight

Isaac loves God. He obeys God. So God gives Isaac many good things. Isaac's Philistine neighbors do not love God. They do not obey God. So God does not give them good things.

The Philistines grow jealous of Isaac. They want the good things God gives him. They do not want Isaac to have them. One day these Philistines fill Isaac's wells with dirt. Now Isaac has no water.

But Isaac will not fight the Philistines. He moves. He digs new wells. But the Philistines steal those wells. Isaac still will not fight them. He moves again. He digs new wells. This time the Philistines do not fill his wells. They do not steal them.

God is pleased with Isaac. He likes
what Isaac has done. "I will give you
many good things," God promises. He
did! Do you like what Isaac did? Do
you like what God did for Isaac?

Jacob Deceives His Father

Jacob and Esau are twin brothers. Esau was born a few minutes before Jacob. He is the older brother. So Esau has the birthright. The oldest boy in each family always received this birthright.

The son with the birthright received
special things when his father died.
He got more of the family money. The
other children thought he was the
most important. He even became the
chief, the leader of the family.

Do you remember when Jacob bought
Esau's birthright? Do you remember
that he traded a bowl of stew for it?
Now Jacob must get his father to give
him the birthright. It isn't really his until
his father says so. But how will he do it?

One day Jacob deceives his father. He
pretends to be Esau. He dresses like
Esau. He smells like Esau. He even
tries to talk like Esau. Isaac thinks
Jacob is Esau. So he gives Esau's
birthright to Jacob.

Jacob Has a Special Dream

Esau was angry when Jacob deceived their father. He even said he would kill Jacob. Jacob is afraid now. He will run away from home. He will go on a long trip far, far from home.

One night Jacob lies down to sleep. He puts his head on a big rock. That is his pillow. How would you like to have a rock for your pillow tonight? As Jacob sleeps with his rock pillow, he has a special dream.

In his special dream Jacob sees a long stairway from earth to heaven. Angels walk up and down on this stairway. Then God speaks to Jacob. "I will do wonderful things for you," God tells Jacob.

Jacob is surprised. God is talking to him. God has not talked to anyone for a long time. What should he say to God? What would you say to God if He talked to you? "I will do wonderful things for You too," Jacob promises God.

Jacob Meets Rachel

Jacob must go far, far away from home.
He is running away from his brother
Esau. Esau was angry because Jacob had
taken his birthright. Esau even said he
would kill Jacob. That would make
anyone run far away, wouldn't it?

But look! Do you see who Jacob sees?
Her name is Rachel. She is beautiful,
isn't she? Jacob thinks Rachel is
beautiful, too. He wants to meet her.
But he must find the right way to do it.

Do you see what Rachel is doing?
Rachel takes care of her father's
sheep. Jacob is helping her give the
sheep water. That is kind for Jacob to
do, isn't it? Do you think Rachel
thinks it is kind too?

Rachel is glad that Jacob has come to this place. She is glad that she can meet Jacob. Someday they will get married. Someday they will have children. God has special plans for Jacob and Rachel.

Joseph's Brothers Sell Him

Joseph's brothers do not like him.
Their father Jacob loves Joseph more
than any of them. He gives Joseph
special gifts. He even gives Joseph a
special coat with many colors. This
makes Joseph's brothers angry.

Joseph's brothers think of ways they can hurt Joseph. Some even plan to kill him. Then one brother has an idea. Why not sell Joseph? Have you ever heard of someone selling his brother?

Some men come to that place. They
want to buy Joseph. They will make
him a slave. So Joseph's brothers sell
him to these men. That is a very bad
thing to do, isn't it?

Joseph's brothers watch the men take him away. They know that Joseph will be a slave. They think he will die because he will work so hard. These are very bad brothers, aren't they?

God Helps Joseph

Joseph is far away from home now.
His brothers sold him to some bad
men. These men who bought Joseph
brought him to Egypt. But a woman
lied about Joseph. She said Joseph did
something bad. But he didn't.

Some men put Joseph in jail. Joseph is so sad. Does anyone care? Can anyone help him now? Then one night the king of Egypt has a strange dream. "Help me know what it means," the king says. But no one can help him.

God tells Joseph what the king's
dream means. Joseph tells the king.
Now the king is very happy. He
knows that God is helping Joseph. So
the king wants Joseph to keep on
helping him.

"You are a wise man," the king tells
Joseph. "Help me rule my people."
The king makes Joseph governor of
Egypt. Joseph will work for the king.
He will rule all the people of Egypt.

Joseph Has a Secret

One day Joseph's brothers come to Egypt.
They do not have food back home. So
they must come to Egypt to buy it. Joseph
is governor of Egypt. He is the ruler of all
the country. Joseph's brothers must buy
their food from the governor.

Joseph's brothers come to see the
governor. But they do not know that
the governor is Joseph. This is
Joseph's secret. Why doesn't Joseph
tell his brothers? He wants to know if
they are sorry that they sold him.

Joseph listens to his brothers. He pretends that he does not know their lan-
guage. So they talk about Joseph.
They say how bad it was to sell
Joseph. Now he knows they are sorry.

Joseph tells his special secret. "I am Joseph," he tells his brothers. Do you think they are surprised? Do you think they are happy?

Hebrew Slaves Work in Egypt

These poor slaves work all day. They
work every day. They are making
bricks. But they do not get paid.
That's because they are slaves. The
King of Egypt owns these slaves.

The king is also mean to his slaves. He
sends mean men to make them work
hard. Sometimes the mean men whip
them. Sometimes they hurt these poor
slaves. Don't you think these slaves
are sad?

But these Hebrew slaves love God.
God loves them too. He gives them
many wonderful children. The
Hebrew slaves love their wonderful
children.

The bad king does not want the slaves to have many children. He is afraid there will be too many Hebrew people. He is afraid they might hurt him. So he plans to kill these Hebrew children.

God Takes Care of Baby Moses

Look! Do you see Baby Moses sleeping? He is sleeping in a basket. His mother made the basket. She hid Baby Moses here in this basket. She hid him from the king and his bad men.

The king is afraid. He thinks the
Hebrews have too many children. He
wants to kill the Hebrew baby boys.
He sent some bad men to do this. If
Baby Moses cries, these bad men may
find him. If they do, they will kill him.

But do you see that lady? She is a
princess. She has found Baby Moses. The
princess wants a baby. She wants to keep
Baby Moses. He will be her baby. She
needs a woman to help her take care of
Baby Moses. But where will the princess
find her?

"I know someone who can help you,"
a little girl says. Miriam is Baby Moses'
big sister. She runs to find their mother.
Now Baby Moses is safe. The king and
his bad men will not hurt him. God is
taking care of him, isn't He?

A Bush Keeps Burning

Moses' people are slaves in Egypt. They
have been slaves there for many years.
But Moses is not there with them. He
went away many years ago. Now Moses
is a shepherd. He takes care of sheep.
Moses often prays for his people.

"Help my people," Moses prays. "Send someone to take them out of Egypt." Moses wants God to send someone else. He does not want God to send him back to Egypt. The king is angry at Moses. He will try to kill Moses.

One day Moses is taking care of the sheep. He sees a bush. The bush is burning. But it does not stop burning. It keeps on burning for a long, long time. Then God talks to Moses. God's voice comes from the burning bush.

"Go back to Egypt," God tells Moses. "Lead your people from Egypt. I will help you. I will show you what to do." Do you think Moses is afraid? He is. But he knows that God is with him.

Ten Terrible Troubles

God tells Moses to go back to Egypt.
He tells Moses to lead His people
away from Egypt. So Moses obeys
God. He goes back to Egypt. Then
Moses goes to see the king. "Let my
people go," Moses tells the king.

The king does not like what Moses says. "No, I will not let the people go," the king tells Moses. "I will keep them as my slaves." Then bad things begin to happen to the king. Bad things begin to happen all over Egypt. God makes these things happen.

Moses comes to see the king many
times. He keeps telling the king to let
the people go. He keeps telling the king
to stop making the people slaves. But
the king keeps saying NO. So God keeps
sending bad things to hurt the king.

94

One night God causes something sad
to happen in Egypt. The oldest boys
die. Even the king's oldest boy dies.
Now the king says YES. At last he
knows that God is greater than his
gods. Now Moses can lead his people
from Egypt.

Moses Leads His People

The King of Egypt is a bad man. He makes Moses' people work hard. But he will not pay them. They are the king's slaves. The king thinks that he owns them. He thinks they should do whatever he wants.

Do you remember the ten bad things that happened? The king remembers them. How can he forget? God sent those ten bad things. Now the king knows that God can do anything. That's why the king lets Moses' people go away.

The people are not slaves now. They
do not work for the king. He does not
own them now. They are going
toward a new land. God promised
them this new land. Moses leads his
people each day. God leads Moses.

Do you think Moses is happy that God leads them? Do you think Moses' people are happy too? "Thank You, God," Moses prays. "Thank You, God," Moses' people pray too.

God Leads Moses and His People

God has promised a special land for Moses' people. Moses will show them how to get there. He leads them each day. But how does Moses know where to go? He has never been to this special land.

"I will show you the way," God promises Moses. God has a special land for the people. So He knows how to get there. He will show Moses which way to go. But Moses must listen to God each day.

Do you see the tall cloud in the sky?
God sent that cloud. It is a special
cloud. Moses does not know the way
to God's Promised Land. But God
knows. Each day He shows Moses
which way to go. Each day Moses follows the cloud that God sent.

It is night now. The tall cloud is not there now. But there is a fire that looks like a cloud. God sends this fire each night. It shows Moses where to go. Now you know why Moses follows that fire.

A Path through a Sea

The king chases Moses and his people. He wants to hurt them. How can they get away from this bad man? They are trapped. The king and his soldiers are behind them and beside them. A sea is in front of them.

"We're trapped! How can we get across the sea?" the people ask. The people do not have boats. They have no way to go across the sea. "God will help us," Moses says. "He will do something wonderful!"

Do you see what is happening? God
sent a wind. It is blowing on the sea. It
is blowing the water apart. Soon there
is a big wall of water on this side.
There is a big wall of water on that
side. But there is a dry path in the
middle of the sea.

Now the people can get across the sea. God did something wonderful, didn't He? Now the people can walk on God's special path. The king tries to chase the people. But the water comes back on the king and his army. God took care of Moses and his people.

God Sends Special Food

Moses and his people are in a desert. There are no stores in the desert. There are no gardens or fields. There are no vineyards. There is no food at all. "We're hungry," the people say. You can see why they are hungry, can't you?

"God will send good food for you,"
Moses tells his people. But how can
He? How can He give them food?
There is no food to give.

But God does send good food. Each
day He sends a special bread. It is
called manna. God does not need
stores. He does not need gardens. God
sends manna as a special gift. God can
do anything, can't He?

Now the people have all they can eat.
The manna is wonderful food. It tastes
good. There is plenty of it. "Thank
You, God," Moses often prays. "Thank
You, God," the people also pray.

God's Ten Commandments

God has some special rules for Moses and his people. He tells Moses to come high up a mountain. There God gives Moses these special rules. God talks with Moses. He tells Moses many wonderful things.

"I want the people to obey My rules," God tells Moses. When people obey God's rules, they obey God. That's a good idea, isn't it? You want to obey God too, don't you?

Moses listens carefully. God writes
some of His rules on stones. He gives
these stones to Moses. Then God tells
Moses more rules. Moses tells the
people what God wants.

Some of the people obey God's rules. They are very happy. But some want to do what THEY want. They do not want to obey God. Those people are not happy. They are very sad.

The Golden Calf

Moses is leading his people through a big desert. He is leading them toward a special land. God promised them this special land. One day Moses goes high up a mountain. God wants to talk to him there.

While Moses is gone, the people make a statue. It is a golden calf. "This statue is our god," they say. "We will worship it instead of God." That is a bad thing to do, isn't it?

Moses comes down from the mountain. He sees the golden calf. He hears what the people are doing. Moses is angry with his people. "You must worship God, not a statue," he says.

Some people listen to Moses. They
want to follow God. That makes them
very happy. But others want to worship the statue. God punishes those
people. Now everyone knows that
God is the One to worship.

Giving for God's House

Moses and his people live in a desert. There are no houses. There are no churches. "God wants us to make a beautiful tent-house for Him," Moses tells the people. God's tent-house can be moved from place to place.

"Give your best things for God's house," Moses tells the people. So the people bring many beautiful gifts. Moses and his people will make God's beautiful house with these gifts.

Do you think these people are happy
to give for God's house? They are.
They keep bringing gifts. They give
and give and give. They give more
than Moses needs.

"Stop bringing your gifts," Moses tells the people. "We have more than we need to make God's house." You can see how much the people want to please God.

God's Beautiful House

Moses and his people gave many beautiful things. They gave these things to make God's tent-house. Now look! Do you see God's beautiful tent-house? It is called the tabernacle.

Moses and some special workmen made the tent-house. They made it the way God said. God planned His house. He told Moses how to build it. Don't you wish you could see the tabernacle?

God's beautiful tent-house has special
furniture inside. It is covered with
gold. There is a gold table. There is a
special gold chest. There are golden
bowls and plates. Even the lamps are
made of gold.

God talks with Moses in the tabernacle. He tells Moses what the people should do. Now God has a special tent-house. Moses and his people take it everywhere they go.

God Gives Meat to Eat

Moses and his people have no meat to eat. They live in a desert. There are no grocery stores. There are no butcher shops. There is no place to get meat. "We want meat to eat," the people grumble.

Moses does not have meat to give
them. What can he do? Will God do
something special for the people? Will
He give special meat to them?

One day God sends special meat from
the sky. Birds called "quail" fly in.
They fly down to the ground. The
people catch the quail.

The people have meat to eat now. God sent the quail. It is His special gift to the people. Do you think they said, "Thank You" to God for His gift?

God Promises a Special Land

"I will give you that special land,"
God tells the people. "Go in and take
it. I will help you." The people have
lived in the desert for many months.
Now it is time to go into the special
land God has promised.

"The people who live there are too big," some people complain. "They are too strong. We can't take the land from them." These people do not believe that God will help them. They do not trust God to give them the land.

"We can take this land," some other
people say. "God will help us. He
promised to give us this land. Let's
take it."

But the other people will not help
them. So Moses and his people must
live in the desert for many more years.
They could have had the beautiful
land God promised. Now they are
very sad.

Joshua Fights for Jericho

Do you see those walls? Joshua sees them. Joshua and his soldiers must go over those walls. They must capture this city called Jericho. But how can they do it? Jericho's soldiers will kill them.

God tells Joshua how to do it. "March around Jericho," God says. "Do it every day. On the seventh day, march around Jericho seven times. Blow on your trumpets! Shout! Then the walls will fall down."

Joshua and his soldiers do what God
said. Each day they march around
Jericho. On the seventh day they
march around it seven times. Then
they blow on their trumpets. They
shout. Look at those walls now!

The walls are falling down. God said
that would happen. Joshua obeyed
God. God did what He promised.
Now Joshua and his soldiers can go
into Jericho. They will take the city.
Joshua is glad he obeyed God. Are
you glad when you obey God too?

Gideon's Little Army

Gideon and his army must fight the Midianites. But Gideon has a little army. The Midianites have a big army. Would you like to fight a big army with a little army? That's what Gideon must do.

God promises to help Gideon. "Light torches," God tells Gideon. "Cover them with pitchers. Tell your soldiers to carry them. Take them near the Midianite camp." Would you like to fight with torches and pitchers?

Gideon and his soldiers do what God says. They know that God will help them. They light torches. They cover them with pitchers. Then they go near the Midianite camp. "Break the pitchers," God says. That's what Gideon and his soldiers do.

Suddenly the Midianites see torches
around their camp. They hear Gideon
and his men shouting. The Midianites
are afraid. They have a big army. But
they think Gideon has a bigger army.
So the Midianites run away. Thank
You, God!

Samson Fights a Lion

How would you like to fight a lion?
How would you like to fight one with
only your hands? Samson did. But
Samson was the strongest man in the
world. That's the way God made him.

One day a lion jumps at Samson. Most people would run. But Samson doesn't run. He grabs the lion. He fights the lion. Do you hear the lion growling? Would you be afraid if you were there?

God helps Samson. He helps Samson
be strong. Now Samson kills the lion.
Samson kills it with his hands. He
does not have a knife. He does not
have a gun. Could you do that?

God really did help Samson, didn't He? God may not want you to fight lions or tigers. But He will help you when you really need Him. Next time you need God's help, ask Him.

Ruth Helps Naomi

Ruth is a beautiful lady. She and
Naomi's son were married. But he
died. Now Ruth lives with Naomi.
Ruth grew up in Moab. But Naomi
grew up in Israel. Now Naomi wants
to go home.

"I will go with you," Ruth tells
Naomi. "You should stay here in
Moab with your people," Naomi says.
Ruth will not know anyone in Israel.
Naomi will be her only friend.

Ruth loves her mother-in-law Naomi.
So Ruth leaves her family and friends
in Moab. She goes with Naomi to
Israel. That was very kind, wasn't it?

Naomi cannot work now. She is too
old. So Ruth works. She gathers grain
for both of them. One day a kind man
sees Ruth. He asks Ruth to marry him.
Now Ruth and Naomi are happy. The
kind man is happy too.

God Talks to Samuel

Samuel lives in God's house. But it is
not like your church. God's house is a
big tent. It is called the tabernacle.
Samuel helps a man take care of God's
house.

Samuel sleeps near a big, golden chest. The chest has stones inside. God wrote ten important rules on these stones. Have you heard of The Ten Commandments? Those are the ten rules God wrote on these stones.

153

One night God talks to Samuel.
Samuel loves God. So Samuel listens
carefully. He wants to know what God
says. You would do that too, wouldn't
you?

God tells Samuel something special.
He tells about some things He will do.
God may never talk to you the way
He talked to Samuel. But He does talk
through His Word. Are you listening?

The People Want a King

The people of Israel do not have a king. God tells Samuel what to say to the people. Then Samuel tells the people. The people do not need a king. God is really their king. Samuel is God's helper.

"We want a king," the people say. "We want to be like other nations." The people know that God is their king. They know that is better than having a king. But they still want a king.

"A king will make you work hard for him," Samuel tells the people. "He will take money from you. He will take the best of your things."

"We still want a king," the people say.
"We want to be like the other
nations." So God tells Samuel, "Let
them have a king." God helps Samuel
find their king. He is a tall man
named Saul.

David Fights a Giant

"Send someone to fight me," Goliath shouts. But the soldiers of Israel are afraid. Goliath is nine feet tall. He is a great soldier. How can anyone fight a giant? King Saul is afraid too. He will not fight Goliath.

"I will fight him," David says. But
David is not a soldier. He isn't even a
big man. He is still a boy. How can he
fight a giant? How can he win? Look!
All David has is a slingshot. Goliath
has a big spear.

"God will help me," David says.
Goliath does not want God's help. He
does not believe in God. He thinks he
is bigger than God. He thinks he does
not need God.

Now look what happens. David wins!
That's because God helped David.
When you need help, remember to ask
God. He will help you.

David and Jonathan Are Friends

Prince Jonathan saw David fight Goliath. He saw David win. He knows that David asked God for help. Prince Jonathan likes David. He wants to be David's friend.

"Will you be my friend?" Jonathan asks David. What do you think David will say? Do you think he will be Jonathan's friend?

Prince Jonathan is giving David good gifts. He is giving David his beautiful robe. He is giving David his sword. He is giving David his belt. He is giving David his bow to shoot arrows. Those are wonderful gifts for David.

David and Jonathan become best friends. They will be friends for a long, long time. You can see why, can't you?

David Is Kind to Mephibosheth

David is king now. He can help people. Or he can hurt people. But David
is a kind king. He wants to help
people.

Do you see Mephibosheth? He is the
one with crutches. He is the son of
Prince Jonathan. Jonathan was
David's best friend before Jonathan
was killed. That's why King David
wants to be kind to Mephibosheth.

David gives Mephibosheth good gifts.
He tells Mephibosheth to live with
him in the palace. Mephibosheth has a
beautiful home now. He has all the
good food he can eat.

Do you think Mephibosheth is
thankful? Do you think he says thank
you to King David? Would you?

King Solomon's Special Gift

Solomon was King David's son. When David died, Solomon became king. One night Solomon has a dream. It is a special dream. God talks to Solomon in the dream.

"I will give you anything you want," God tells King Solomon. What would you want? Solomon can ask for money. He can ask to be powerful or famous. He can ask for anything. God said He would give it.

"Help me be a wise king," Solomon prays. "Help me rule my people well." Solomon does not ask for money. He does not ask for power. He does not ask to be famous.

"I will make you wise," God says. So Solomon becomes a very wise man. "I will also make you rich and famous. I will give you great power." Do you think Solomon asked for the right gifts?

King Solomon Builds God's House

King Solomon loves God. He wants to make a special house for God. People will come to God's house. They will talk with God there. They will sing to God too.

God's house will be very beautiful. It will be more beautiful than the king's house. Solomon will tell many workers to put God's house together. They will make it with many beautiful things.

God's house is called a temple. It is the most beautiful building in the land. "Come to God's house," the king tells the people. So people come from all over the land. They want to be together in God's house.

King Solomon prays at God's house.
The people sing songs about God. The
people know that God is there. So
they want to be there too. That's why
they pray and sing songs. Do you like
to pray and sings songs in God's
house too?

Ravens Give Elijah Good Food

"Where will I get food to eat?" Elijah asks. Elijah is God's helper. He is hungry. Everyone else is hungry too. There is almost no food in the land. That's because it has not rained for a long time.

"Go to the river where I show you,"
God tells Elijah. "I will send ravens
with food for you." Can God do that?
Can He send birds with food? Elijah
knows he must obey God. Then God
will take care of him.

Elijah goes to the place where God said. Each day God sends ravens. Each morning the ravens bring food for Elijah. Each evening they bring more food for him.

God takes care of His helper. Elijah
has all the food he needs. "Thank You,
God," Elijah prays. "Thank You for
taking good care of me." Does God
take care of you too? Do you remember to thank Him?

God Helps a Poor Woman and Elijah

"Go to a little village," God tells Elijah. "You will find a poor widow there. She will give you food." But how can a poor widow give food? She does not have enough food for herself and her son.

Elijah does what God said. He knows
that he must obey God. Elijah goes to
the little village. He finds the poor
widow. She is picking up sticks.

"Give me something to eat," Elijah asks. "I have only a little flour," the woman tells him. "I can bake some bread for me and my son. That is all we have. We will have no food after that." But the poor woman shares her food with Elijah.

"God will give you plenty of food,"
Elijah tells the woman. He does! Each
day the woman takes flour from her
jar. She makes more bread. Each day
there is always enough flour for
tomorrow. "God sent you to help us,"
she says.

Is God Really God?

"Baal is God!" some foolish men say. They believe this statue is God. They want other people to believe this too. They should know that a statue cannot be God.

"God is God," some other people say.
They know that God made the whole
world. He made everything in it. He
made everyone in it. They know that
people made the Baal statue. But the
Baal statue never made any people.

One day Elijah meets these foolish
men. "We will find out who really is
God," Elijah says. "The true God will
send fire from heaven." Elijah makes a
stone altar. He puts meat on the altar.
He pours water on it.

"Ask Baal to send fire," Elijah tells the men. They beg Baal to do that. But a statue can't send fire. It cannot even hear them. Elijah asks God to send fire. Do you see that fire? Everyone knows now that God is really God. You know that too, don't you?

A Room for God's Helper

Elisha is God's helper. He goes from place to place doing God's work. "Eat with us when you come to town," a man and woman tell him. So Elisha does. He likes to go to their house.

One day the man and woman have a surprise for Elisha. "Look at this beautiful room," they tell him. "We made it for you. Stay here when you come to our town."

This is a beautiful upstairs bedroom.
The man and woman put a table in it.
They put a lamp and chair in it. And
they put a bed in it too.

"Thank you for the beautiful room,"
Elisha says. "Thank you for doing
God's work," the man and woman tell
him. Do you like to help God's
helpers? That's a good thing to do,
isn't it?

195

A Big Chest Full of Money

"We must fix God's house," King Joash says. God's house needs to be fixed. People have not taken care of it. They have not cleaned it. That's why it is a mess. "But we need money to fix God's house," the workers say.

King Joash has an idea. "Make a big
chest," he says. "Put it at the gate of
God's house." The men do what the
king says. They make a hole in the top
of the chest. People can now put
money through the hole.

Do you see what the people are doing? They are putting money into the chest. The money will be used to fix God's house. The people want to do this. They do not want God's house to be a mess.

Now the king and his helpers can fix God's house. They will hire men to do the work. Soon God's house will be beautiful. Do you think this will please God?

Nehemiah Builds Some Walls

Jerusalem was once a beautiful city. But some soldiers came. They knocked down the walls. They burned the city. They took the people away to another land. For many years the city was left torn down. The people lived far away.

"Please let me go home," Nehemiah asks the king one day. "Please let me build the walls of Jerusalem again." Nehemiah is the king's special helper. The king likes Nehemiah.

The king lets Nehemiah go to
Jerusalem. He lets Nehemiah build the
walls again. Nehemiah asks some men
to help him. Others try to stop them.
But God helps Nehemiah. He keeps
on building the walls.

Soon the walls are built. The city
is beautiful again. "Thank You, God,"
Nehemiah prays. Remember to thank
God when He helps you.

A Beautiful Queen

Queen Esther is the most beautiful lady in the land. The king thinks so. That's why he married Esther. He loves Esther too.

Haman is one of the king's helpers.
But he is a bad man. He wants to kill
all the Jewish people. He makes plans
to kill them. But he must trick the
king. The king must let him kill these
people.

The king does not know that Esther is Jewish. Haman does not know this either. One day Esther tells the king that Haman's plan will kill her. The king is angry. He loves Esther. He will not let this happen.

The king punishes Haman. Now
Queen Esther is happy. She has saved
her life. But she has also saved her
people. Do you think she thanked
God? Would you?

Bad News and Good News for Job

One day Job has some bad news. "Men have killed some of your helpers," a man says. "They stole everything there." Then another man has more bad news. "Fire burned all your sheep and shepherds," he says.

208

Another man comes to Job. He has
more bad news. "More men came and
killed your other helpers," he says.
Then another man comes with more
bad news. "Your children have all
been killed," he says. Then Job gets
terrible sores all over him.

Poor Job! What will he do? Satan said he would curse God. But God said he would not. What do you think he will do?

Job does not get angry at God. He
does not curse God. "God gave me all
I have," Job says. "I will still love
Him." God is pleased with Job. So He
gives Job much more than he had
before. Do you think Job thanked God
for helping him?

Daniel Does Not Eat the King's Food

An army comes to Daniel's land.
Daniel's people fight the army. But the
army wins. The soldiers take Daniel
and his friends. They take them far
away to another land.

Daniel and his friends must help their
new king. "We will show you what to
do," a man says. "But you must eat
what the king eats." The food is wonderful food. But it has been offered to
the king's gods before it is served.

Daniel and his friends do not want to eat the king's food. God will not be pleased. "Please let us eat other food," Daniel asks. The man likes Daniel. He lets Daniel and his friends eat other food.

God takes care of Daniel and his friends. They grow strong. They grow wise. They are good helpers for the king. So the king is pleased. God is pleased too.

Daniel and Some Hungry Lions

Daniel loves God. Each day he prays to God. It is not easy. Most of Daniel's neighbors do not believe in God. Some do not want Daniel to pray to God. They want to hurt Daniel.

Some bad men think of a way to hurt
Daniel. They make a new rule. A person can pray only to the king. The bad
men trick the king. He thinks it is a
good rule. He makes everyone
follow the rule.

The king likes Daniel. He does not
know this rule will hurt Daniel. But
the bad men know it. If Daniel prays,
he can be thrown into a den of hungry
lions. Will Daniel stop praying now?
Would you?

Daniel will not stop praying. So the
bad men catch him. They put him in
the den of hungry lions. But God will
not let the lions hurt Daniel. Now the
king knows that God helps Daniel. He
punishes those bad men. Aren't you
glad God helped Daniel?

A Big Fish Swallows Jonah

"Go to Nineveh," God tells Jonah. "Tell them that I have sent you." God has bad news for Nineveh. The people are not pleasing Him. They are very bad people. Jonah is afraid. What will those bad people do to him? Will they hurt him?

Jonah runs away. He is on a ship. He
tries to run away from God. He is
afraid to go to Nineveh. But you can't
run away from God, can you? God
knows that Jonah is on that ship. He
sees Jonah. So God sends a big storm.

Big waves crash against Jonah's ship.
The sailors are afraid. This is a terrible
storm. "Why is this happening?" they
ask. "Because I am running away
from God," Jonah tells them. So the
sailors throw Jonah into the sea.

But look! There is a big fish. God made that fish. He sent the fish to swallow Jonah. Jonah is inside the fish for three days. The fish spits Jonah onto some land. NOW do you think Jonah will go to Nineveh? Or will he try to run away again?

An Angel Has Good News for Mary

Look at that angel! Mary has never seen an angel before. Have you? "Don't be afraid," the angel says. Would you be afraid? This angel has good news for Mary. God has told the angel what to say.

"You will have a special baby," the
angel says. "He is God's Son. You will
call Him Jesus." "But how can I have
a baby?" Mary asks. "I don't have a
husband yet." "God will be the baby's
Father," says the angel. "Will you let
Him do this?"

"I will do what God wants me to do," Mary says. The angel is pleased to hear Mary say this. Do you think God is pleased too? He is!

Now the angel is gone. Mary is alone. Do you think she thanks God for His good news? Would you like to thank God now for sending Jesus?

Baby Jesus

Look! Do you see the baby? He is sleeping. Mary and Joseph are taking care of Him. Baby Jesus was born in this stable. That is a place where animals eat and sleep. Do you think the animals were glad to see Baby Jesus?

Do you see the animals? They see Baby Jesus. They are very quiet. They know this is a special baby. Do you think they know that God sent Him? Do you think they know that He is God's Son?

It is night now. The people of
Bethlehem are sleeping. God's Son
came to their town tonight. The people do not know that. But Mary and
Joseph know. God told them.

You know that Baby Jesus is God's Son. The Bible tells you so. Would you like to say, "Thank You, God"? Would you like to say that now? "Thank You, God, for sending Baby Jesus."

Shepherds Visit Baby Jesus

Shhh. The sheep are sleeping. It is night now. The sky is dark. But it is full of bright stars. Do you see the shepherds? They are taking care of the sheep. They will keep wild animals from hurting the sheep.

Look! What is that bright light in the sky? Is it an angel? It IS an angel! The angel is talking to the shepherds. "Good News!" the angel says. God's Son is born tonight in Bethlehem."

Look! Now there are many angels.
The sky is filled with them. They are
singing. They are praising God. What
a beautiful sight. Have you ever seen
hundreds of angels singing? The shepherds have never seen that either.

Now the angels are gone. The sky is dark again. The stars twinkle. All is quiet. "Let's go to Bethlehem," the shepherds say. Would you like to go with them?

Wise Men Bring Gifts for Jesus

"A great king is born," the wise men say. "We must follow that special star. It will show us how to find Him." The wise men leave their homes. They ride their camels every night. They follow the special star.

The special star goes all the way to Bethlehem. The wise men follow it there. "The great King is here!" they say. Do you think God sent that special star?

The wise men have wonderful gifts
for the new King. They have gold.
They also have spices. The spices are
called frankincense and myrrh. These
gifts cost lots of money.

The wise men give their special gifts
to little Jesus. They bow down to this
new King. That makes them very
happy. Are you happy when you give
good gifts to Jesus? Are you happy
when you show your love to Him?

Go to Egypt!

One night an angel talks to Joseph. He has something special to tell him. "Get up!" the angel says. "Take Jesus and Mary with you. Run away to Egypt. The king wants to kill Jesus."

Joseph listens. He knows that he must obey. God tells the angel what to say. Soldiers will come to their house. They will try to kill Jesus. He must go to Egypt tonight.

Joseph puts Mary and Jesus on the
donkey. They leave that night on their
long trip. They ride all the way to
Egypt. God will take care of them in
Egypt. He will keep the bad king from
hurting little Jesus.

242

So little Jesus lived in Egypt. The bad
king will not hurt Him here. God will
take care of Him. Thank You, God, for
taking care of little Jesus. Thank You,
God, for taking care of me.

The Boy Jesus

Do you see that boy? He is Jesus! He is making things from wood. Joseph has a carpenter shop. Jesus helps him each day. Jesus is learning how to be a carpenter.

Joseph makes many things from
wood. Jesus watches him. Jesus helps
him. Joseph is glad he can take care of
Jesus. He is glad he can help Jesus
learn to be a carpenter.

Jesus is growing up in a little town. It is called Nazareth. Mary takes care of Him. Joseph takes care of Him too. They know they are helping God take care of Him.

Thank You, God, for taking care of the
boy Jesus. Thank You, God, for taking
care of me.

Jesus Teaches Some Teachers

One day Jesus goes with Mary and Joseph to Jerusalem. People come from all over the land. They eat together. They talk together. They go to God's house together. This special time together is called the Passover.

248

Mary and Joseph start home with a big crowd of people. Suddenly they see that Jesus is not with them. They thought He was with uncles or aunts or cousins. But He isn't there. Where is He?

Mary and Joseph hurry back to
Jerusalem. They look everywhere. At
last they look in God's house. Jesus is
there, teaching some teachers. Most
boys don't teach teachers. But Jesus
does.

"How does this boy know so much about God?" the teachers ask. You know, don't you? Jesus lived with God in heaven. He knows all about God. That's why we should listen to Him too.

John, the Preacher

What kind of clothes does your preacher wear? John wears camelhair cloth with a wide belt. What kind of food does your preacher eat? John eats locusts and wild honey. Locusts are like grasshoppers. Would you like grasshoppers for dinner?

Where does your preacher preach? In
a beautiful church? Behind a beautiful
pulpit? John preaches in the desert.
He has no church. He has no pulpit.
He has no choir or organ. There are no
chairs where people can sit.

Many people listen to John. He preaches about sin. He tells people about God. God wants to forgive their sin.

Some people want to follow God.
They want to please God. John is glad
that he can preach to them. Some of
them will live in heaven forever. John
has told them how to get there.

John Baptizes Jesus

John is a preacher. He tells people how to please God. "I want to please God," some people say. "I will baptize you," John tells them. Then he baptizes them in the Jordan River.

Many people come to hear John
preach. Many want John to baptize
them. They want to please God. That
is the way they can tell others. Do you
think John baptizes them?

One day Jesus comes to see John. "Baptize Me," Jesus tells him. "I want to please God too." That is one way Jesus can tell others that He pleases God.

John baptizes Jesus. When he does, God speaks from heaven. "This is My Son," God says. "He really does please Me." Do you really please God too?

Satan Tempts Jesus

Here is Jesus. Do you see Him? He has been in this lonely place for 40 days. Jesus isn't really alone. God is with Him. God will take care of Him, even in this lonely place.

Jesus is hungry. Do you know why? He has not had breakfast for 40 days. He has not had lunch for 40 days. He has not had dinner for 40 days. He has had nothing to eat for 40 days. Would you be hungry too?

One day Satan comes to see Jesus. He
wants to tempt Jesus. He wants Jesus
to obey him instead of God. If He
does, Jesus cannot do God's work. He
cannot be our Savior if He obeys
Satan. But Jesus does not obey Satan.

"I must obey God," Jesus tells Satan.
"I must do what God's Word says. I
cannot obey you." Do you want to
obey God too? Don't listen to Satan
when he tempts you. Don't obey
Satan. Obey God! That will please
Him.

Nicodemus Visits Jesus

One night Nicodemus comes to see
Jesus. "God sent you," he tells Jesus.
Nicodemus is an important teacher.
He knows much about God. But Jesus
knows more. That's because Jesus
lives with God in heaven.

"You must be born again," Jesus tells Nicodemus. Nicodemus is surprised. "How can I do that?" he asks. "Can I be born from my mother again?"

Then Jesus tells Nicodemus what He means. We are born once as a baby. Each of us becomes a person here on earth. But we must be born again. This time God makes us new persons. He makes us ready to live in heaven.

Nicodemus listens carefully. He is a great teacher. But he is also a great learner. He learns something important about going to heaven. What did you learn about this?

A Woman at a Well

Do you see Jesus? He is sitting by a well. "Please give Me a drink," Jesus asks a woman. The woman has a water pot. She has pulled water from the well.

The woman knows Jesus is a special
person. She asks Him many questions.
Jesus tells the woman many
wonderful things. Then Jesus tells her
that He is God's Son. The woman is
excited when she hears that.

The woman runs back to her village. "Come and see a special man," she says. "Can this be God's Son?" People run from the village to see Jesus. Wouldn't you run to see Jesus too?

What do you think Jesus will say to these people? What do you think they will ask God's Son? What would you like to ask Jesus?

Jesus Goes Fishing

Peter and his friends are fishermen.
They catch fish for a living.
Sometimes they catch many fish.
Sometimes they fish all night and do
not catch one fish.

"Let's go fishing," Jesus says one day.
"We fished all night," Peter tells Jesus.
"But we didn't catch one fish." Who
wants to go fishing again? Would
you? But Peter also wants to please
Jesus.

"You will catch fish now," Jesus tells him. So Peter and his friends go with Jesus. "Put your nets over there," Jesus says. Peter and his friends throw their nets into the water. They put the nets where Jesus said.

The water is filled with fish. The nets are filled too. Do you see all those fish? Jesus made that happen. Only God's Son can do that. Peter knows that Jesus is God's Son. Do you?

Jesus Calls Some Helpers

Do you remember all those fish Peter and his friends caught? Their boats were full of fish. Now Peter is afraid. "Who is Jesus?" he wonders. "If He can tell fish what to do, He must be God's Son." What would you think if you were Peter?

"Don't be afraid of Me," Jesus says. "I have new work for you. Come with Me. Help Me do God's work." Peter and his friends must stop fishing. They must spend all their time with Jesus. They must help Him every day. Will they do it?

Peter and his friends stop fishing.
They leave their boats and nets. They
go with Jesus. They will be His
helpers.

Now Jesus has four good helpers.
Peter and Andrew are His new
helpers. So are James and John. Jesus
will teach them many good things.
They will help Jesus do God's work.
Will you?

Through the Roof

Jesus did many wonderful things. He healed sick people. He chased demons from people. These were called miracles. You can see why sick people came to see Him.

One day Jesus is in a house. Crowds
are all around Him. Then four men
bring a sick friend. They are carrying
him on a cot. "Please let us in," they
shout. But there are too many people.
They can't get in.

"What will we do?" the men ask. Then they have an idea. The four men take their friend up on the roof. They pull some of the straw away. Now there is a big hole. The men let their friend down beside Jesus.

"Please heal him," they ask Jesus. "I will," Jesus tells them. Do you think the four friends thanked Jesus? Would you?

Jesus Asks Matthew to Be His Helper

No one likes Matthew. He is a tax collector. Matthew makes people pay taxes. He works for the Romans. Matthew's people hate the Romans. They captured this land. Sometimes the Romans are mean to the people there.

You can see why people do not like
Matthew. But Jesus likes him. He
wants Matthew to be His helper.

One day Jesus talks to Matthew.
"Come and be My helper," Jesus says.
"Follow Me." Matthew does not know
what to do. He makes lots of money. If
he follows Jesus, he will make no
money. What would you do?

Matthew leaves his good job. He wants to help Jesus do God's work. That is much more important than money. Matthew is happy to help Jesus. Are you?

Jesus Chooses Twelve Helpers

"I want twelve of you to help Me," Jesus says. He has special work for these twelve. Jesus will teach them how to work for God. He will show them how to choose helpers too.

There are many helpers with Jesus.
Which twelve will He choose? Do you
know? He will call these the Twelve
Apostles. Sometimes they are called
the Disciples. They will help Jesus in
many special ways.

Here are their names. Do you remember Simon Peter, Andrew, James, and John? Do you remember Matthew, the tax collector? Jesus also chooses Philip, Thomas, Thaddeus, and Bartholomew. There is also another Simon and another James. And there is Judas Iscariot.

"Thank You, Jesus," the twelve men say. "Thank You for letting us be Your special helpers." Are you Jesus' helper? Do you like to help Him do God's work? Have you thanked Him for that? Will you?

Jesus Preaches on a Mountain

One day Jesus goes high up a mountain. Many people go up with Him. They want to listen to Jesus. He will have something special to say. He will tell the people about God.

Would you like to listen to Jesus too?
Do you wish you could be on that
mountain with Him? You can't do
that. But you can read what He says
in the Bible.

"Blessed are you," Jesus tells the people. People are happy when they are blessed. God does special things for them. So Jesus tells the people how to be blessed.

Jesus tells us we must be like Him. We must do what He would do. We must do what He says. When we do that, we are blessed, or happy. Would you like to be like Jesus? Would you like to do what He says? You will be happy when you do.

A Widow's Boy Lives Again

Do you see that poor woman? She is crying. She is so sad. Her boy has died. Those people will bury him. The poor woman is alone now. She has no one else to take care of her.

Do you see what I see? Jesus is coming. Can He help this poor woman? What can He do for her? What can anyone do now?

"Don't cry," Jesus tells the poor
woman. Jesus touches the boy's coffin.
"Get up!" Jesus says to the boy. But
how can a dead boy get up?

Look! The boy IS getting up. He was
dead. But Jesus has made him alive
again. That's why the woman is not
crying now. You can see how happy
she is. Would you be happy too if you
were the woman?

Jesus Tells Wonderful Stories

Would you like to hear Jesus tell wonderful stories? You can't listen to His voice. But you can read His stories in the Bible. When Jesus was on earth, everyone wanted to hear Him. They wanted to hear His wonderful stories.

One day Jesus is standing on the
beach. He is standing near the water
of the lake. People crowd closer and
closer to hear Him. Please, people,
don't push Jesus into the water!

Jesus gets into a boat. He pushes the
boat into the water. Now He can tell
stories to the people. They cannot
push Him into the water.

Jesus tells many wonderful stories.
His stories tell us about God. They tell
us about heaven. They tell us how we
should live for God. Jesus' stories are
wonderful stories, aren't they?

Stop, Storm!

"Let's go to the other side of the lake," Jesus says. Jesus and His friends get into a boat. They sail across the big lake. Suddenly the wind begins to blow. Look at those big waves. They are getting higher and higher.

Jesus' friends are afraid. But Jesus isn't afraid. He is sleeping in the back of the boat. "Wake up!" Jesus' friends shout. "Help us! We'll drown!"

But what can Jesus do? What can He say that will make His friends feel better?

"Stop, storm!" Jesus says. Have you ever tried to stop a storm? Would the storm obey you? The storm stops. It obeys Jesus. Even a storm obeys God's Son. You want to obey Jesus too, don't you?

Jesus Helps Jairus' Daughter

"Please come to my house," Jairus begs. "My daughter is sick. Please help her." Jairus is an important man. But he cannot heal his daughter. Can Jesus do that? What do you think?

Jesus goes with Jairus. But it is too
late. Do you see those people crying?
Jairus' daughter has already died.
How can Jesus heal her now? You
know how sad Jairus and his wife
must be.

Jesus makes all the people go away.
Then He talks to Jairus' daughter.
"Get up, little girl," He says. What do
you think the girl will do? How can a
dead girl get up?

But she does! Jairus' daughter gets up.
She is alive again. Can you make a
dead person alive again? Can anyone
do that? Jesus can. That's because He
is God's Son. Only God's Son can do
that.

Lunch for 5,000

How would you like to make lunch for 5,000 people? That's a lot of lunch, isn't it? But Jesus did that. This is the way it happened.

One day Jesus is teaching a big crowd.
There are 5,000 people. One is a little
boy. He has five loaves of bread. He
also has two fish. "May I have your
lunch?" Jesus asks the little boy.

The boy gladly gives his lunch to
Jesus. Then Jesus begins to break the
bread and fish. He keeps on breaking
pieces from them. He keeps on giving
bread and fish to the people. At last
the people have all they can eat.

But bread and fish are left over. Jesus'
friends pick up twelve baskets full of
bread and fish. Could you feed 5,000
people with five loaves and two fish?
Jesus did.

Jesus Walks on Water

Those men are in trouble. The wind is blowing. Big waves are tossing their boat. They are afraid their boat will sink. What will they do? Who can help them?

"Help!" the men shout. But the wind keeps on blowing. The waves keep on tossing their boat. How can anyone help them now? Will their boat sink?

Look! Someone is walking toward
them. He is walking on the water.
How can anyone do that? Who is He?
Now we can see. It is Jesus. He is
walking on the water. He is coming
toward them.

Jesus gets into the boat. Stop, wind!
Stop, waves! Be quiet. The wind sighs
and stops. The waves obey Jesus like a
little lamb. The water is quiet now.
Jesus' friends know now that He is
God's Son. Who else can make the
wind and waves obey?

Jesus Is Our Good Shepherd

Do you know what a shepherd does? He takes care of sheep. A good shepherd loves his sheep. He keeps wild animals from hurting them. He feeds them. He gives them water to drink.

A good shepherd finds a safe place for his sheep. He watches them. He will not leave them alone. A good shepherd wants to help his sheep all the time.

"I am your Good Shepherd," Jesus
says. He is our Good Shepherd too.
He is always there to help us. He
helps us do good things. He helps us
get good food. He helps us find a safe
place to sleep.

Thank You, Jesus, for loving me.
Thank You, for taking good care of
me. Thank You, for being with me all
the time. Thank You, for keeping me
safe. I love You, Jesus.

Mary and Martha Are Jesus' Friends

"Jesus is coming." Mary and Martha
are always happy to see Jesus. They
live with their brother Lazarus. They
live in a little town called Bethany.
When Jesus comes to town He always
stops to see them.

Martha is running here and there. She
wants to make dinner for Jesus. It
must be the best dinner ever. Mary
sits down to talk with Jesus. She asks
Him many questions. Jesus tells her
about God. He tells her about heaven.
It is wonderful!

Martha does not like this. "Tell Mary
to help me get dinner," she says. "I'm
doing all the work." She thinks Mary
is lazy. She thinks Mary does not want
to help. But Jesus knows that is not
true. Mary wants to hear about God
and heaven.

"It is more important to talk about God than eat dinner," Jesus tells Martha. What would you do if you could be with Jesus? Would you rather eat dinner? Or would you rather listen to Him talk about God and heaven?

Finding Lost Sheep

Do you see the shepherd? He takes
care of his sheep. He has 100 sheep.
That is a lot of sheep to feed, isn't it?
But the shepherd loves his sheep. So
he loves to take care of them.

Something is wrong! The shepherd counts his sheep. He does not have 100 sheep now. He has only 99. One of them is lost. Where can that poor lost lamb be? What should the shepherd do?

The shepherd knows what he must do. He looks and looks and looks for his little lost lamb. There it is! At last the shepherd finds his little lost lamb. The shepherd is so happy. You would be happy too, wouldn't you?

"I love you, little lamb," the shepherd says. "I love you like a little lost lamb," Jesus says. "I am so happy when I help you find God." Aren't you glad Jesus loves you so much?

A Boy Who Ran Away

Once there was a man who had two sons. The man has a beautiful home. He has lots of money. The man and his sons have all they need. Do you think they should be happy? Do you think they should want more?

But one boy is not happy. He wants more. "Give me some money," the boy says. "I want to go away. I want to see the world."

The father is sad. He thought the boy
had everything he could want. But he
gives the boy some money. The boy
goes far away. He spends all his
money. Now the boy is hungry. Now
the boy wishes he could go home.

One day the boy goes home. He runs
to his father. "Forgive me, Father," he
begs. "Please let me come home." The
father does forgive him. He lets the
boy come home. God is like that. He
forgives us, even when we do things
wrong. Ask Him! Will you do it now?

Lazarus Comes Back to Life

One day a man comes to see Jesus.
"Lazarus is sick," he tells Jesus.
Lazarus is Jesus' friend. He lives with
his sisters Mary and Martha. They live
in a little town called Bethany.

Jesus goes to Bethany to see Lazarus.
But it takes a long time. It is far away.
Do you see Mary and Martha? They
are glad Jesus has come. But they are
crying. Lazarus has died. They are so
sad.

Do you see that big stone? Lazarus is
buried behind it. "Take that stone
away," Jesus says. Then Jesus shouts.
"Lazarus! Come out of there!" Look!
Lazarus is not dead now. Jesus made
him come back to life.

You can see how happy Mary and
Martha are. They are not crying now.
Only God's Son can make a dead person live again. Aren't you glad Jesus
is God's Son? Aren't you glad He is
your friend?

Ten Men with Leprosy

Do you see those men? There are ten
of them. They have a terrible disease.
It is called leprosy. They are very sick.
They have terrible sores. You can see
how sad they are.

People with leprosy could not live
with their families. They could not be
near friends. They could not touch
anyone. Nobody wanted them near.
They had to live away from home.

"Please help us," the men beg. "Please take our leprosy away." Can Jesus do that? He does! Jesus tells them they are well. Their disease is gone. They are clean.

One man bows down to Jesus. "Thank You, thank You, thank You," he says. The man is so thankful that Jesus has healed him. But where are the others? Why don't they thank Jesus too? Remember to thank Jesus each day! Will you?

Jesus Loves Children

"Touch my child. Pray for my child."
Parents are bringing their children to
Jesus. They want Him to say something special. They want Him to pray
for their children. Do you think He
will?

"He's too busy," say some friends.
"He's too important," say some
others. You know how sad the parents
are. You know how sad the children
are too.

"Stop! Let the children come to Me,"
Jesus says. "People must be like these
children to get to heaven." That makes
children very important, doesn't it?

The children run to Jesus. They hug Him. They talk with Him. They tell Him how much they love Him. Do you think He tells them how much He loves them? Would you like to tell Jesus that you love Him? Would you like to do it now?

A Blind Man Named Bartimeus

A blind man sits by the road. He hears that Jesus is coming. "Jesus, help me," he cries out. "Be quiet," the people shout at him. But Bartimeus keeps on crying out to Jesus. "Help me! Help me!"

Blind people had to beg for money in Jesus' time. Some kind people gave money. Some did not. That was all they had. They could not work. They did not get other help. All they could do was beg.

"Bring the blind man to Me," says Jesus. Bartimeus jumps up and runs to Jesus. "What do you want Me to do?" Jesus asks Bartimeus. "I want to see," says Bartimeus.

"Now you can see," Jesus tells him.
Bartimeus is not blind now. He sees.
He is so happy. "Thank You, thank
You," he shouts. Then He follows
Jesus.

Zacchaeus Climbs a Tree

Zacchaeus was a little man. He was also a tax collector. People hated tax collectors then. They cheated when they took tax money. They gave it to the Romans. The Romans ruled their land.

One day Zacchaeus hears that Jesus is coming to town. He runs to see Him. But there is a big crowd around Jesus. Zacchaeus is too short. He cannot see Jesus. What can he do?

Zacchaeus knows what he can do. He climbs a sycamore tree. Now he can see Jesus. Jesus can see him too. Do you see Zacchaeus?

"Come down," Jesus says. "I will go to your house today." Some people do not like that. They do not want Jesus to go to a tax collector's house. But Zacchaeus wants to know God too. Aren't you glad Jesus loves everyone?

Jesus Rides into Jerusalem

"Bring that donkey to Me," Jesus tells His friends. They bring the donkey to Jesus. They put their cloaks on the donkey. Do you see Jesus riding the donkey? He will ride into Jerusalem.

Crowds of people come. They spread
their cloaks on the ground. They put
palm branches on the ground. They
want Jesus to ride on the cloaks and
branches. "Praise God," people shout.
"Jesus is our king."

"Stop them," some men shout. They do not want people to think Jesus is king. "I will not stop them," Jesus says. "If I do, the stones will shout."

Jesus is a king, isn't He? He does not
want to be king over Jerusalem. He
does not want to be king over the
land. Jesus is God's Son. He is called
King of kings. He is over all the kings
of all the earth. He's very important,
isn't He?

A Woman's Special Gift

Do you see that poor woman? Jesus sees her. Jesus' friends see her too. The poor woman is giving money at God's house. She is giving two little coins. That's not much to give, is it?

Do you see those rich men? Jesus sees them. Jesus' friends see them too. The rich men are giving money at God's house. They are giving many, many big coins. That's a lot to give, isn't it?

"The poor woman is giving more than the rich men," Jesus says. His friends are surprised. How can two little coins be more than many big coins? What does Jesus mean?

"The poor woman is giving all she has," Jesus tells His friends. "The rich men have MUCH left. That is why she is giving more than they." Jesus wants us to give our best to Him. You will, won't you?

The Last Supper

This is a special supper. It is the last supper Jesus will eat with His friends. You can see why it is important, can't you? It is also called a Passover supper. That was a special supper people ate together.

Look at Jesus. He is breaking some
bread. He will give a piece to each
friend. "Eat this," He says. "It will
help you remember Me." Now Jesus
gives a cup to His friends. "Drink
this," He says. "It will help you
remember Me."

365

"Remember how I will die for you,"
Jesus tells His friends. "Remember
that when you eat a piece of bread.
Remember that when you drink from
the cup."

Do you have communion in your church? People remember Jesus when they eat the communion bread. They remember Jesus when they drink from the cup. We remember how He died for us. "Thank You, Jesus, for doing that. I love You."

Jesus Prays in a Garden

After the Last Supper, Jesus and His friends go to a beautiful garden. It is called Gethsemane. There are big olive trees. There are other beautiful plants. And there is a big rock.

"Wait here," Jesus says to three
friends. "I must go over there and
pray." Jesus goes to the big rock. He
bows His head. He begins to pray.
Would you like to hear Jesus pray?
Listen!

"Father, help Me do what You want," Jesus prays. Jesus will soon die on the cross. People will hurt Him terribly. Jesus does not want to suffer. But He wants to please God. You want to do that too, don't you?

"Lord, help Me do what You want."
Have you ever prayed the prayer that
Jesus prayed? Would you like to say
that to God? Would you like to do that
now?

Jesus Dies on the Cross

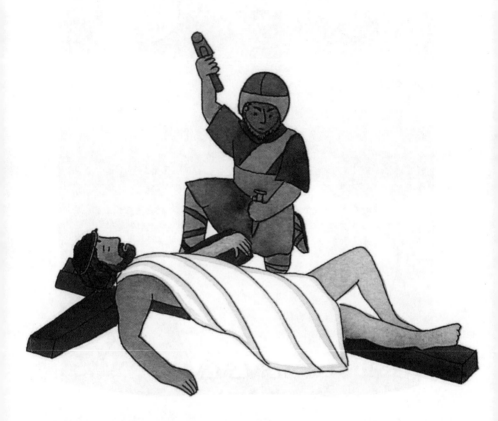

Look! Do you see what some men are
doing to Jesus? They are nailing His
hands to a big wooden cross. They are
nailing His feet too. Jesus has not hurt
these men. But look what they are
doing to Him. Why are they so mean?

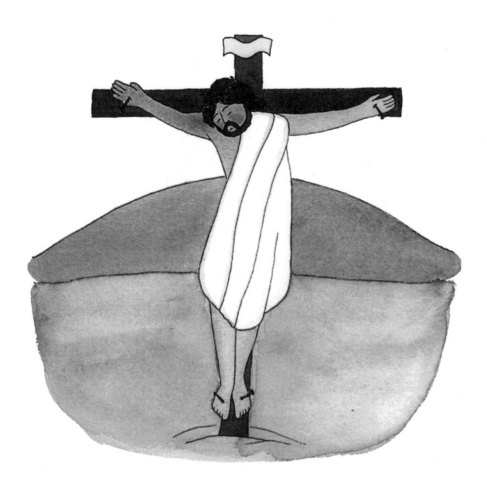

Jesus is dying on the cross. He came
to earth to do this. That's because He
loves us so much. Jesus is punished
for our sin. That doesn't seem fair,
does it? But Jesus wants to do that.

Jesus wants us to live with God in heaven. When we sin, we can't go to heaven. There must be some way to take our sin away.

That is why Jesus is dying on the cross. That is God's way. He is letting Jesus be punished instead of us. Now Jesus wants to be our Savior. Will you ask Him? Now?

Jesus Has Risen!

It is early morning. Some women have come to Jesus' tomb. They want to put spices on His body. That's what people did then. "But how will we roll the big stone from the tomb?" they ask. They can't do it. Who will?

Look! The stone is rolled away. There is an angel. Do you see it? The angel talks to the women. Listen. Can you hear what the angel says?

"He has risen!" the angel says. "Jesus is alive again! Come and see where His body was lying." The women are very surprised. But then they remember. Jesus said that He would do this.

There is another angel. "Go and tell His other friends," the angel says. The women run! They can't wait to tell Jesus' friends that He is alive. Are you excited to tell your friends that too?

Jesus Goes Back to Heaven

Jesus and His friends are walking to the top of a mountain. It is called the Mount of Olives. "The Holy Spirit will come soon," Jesus tells them. "Then you will tell people everywhere about Me."

380

Jesus' friends listen carefully. Then
Jesus lifts His hands. He says some
good things that will happen to them.
Suddenly Jesus begins to rise. His feet
leave the ground. He is rising up
toward the sky.

Jesus' friends watch. They are very
surprised to see this happen. They
watch Jesus go all the way into the
sky. He goes all the way back to
heaven.

Suddenly two angels are standing there. "Jesus has gone back to heaven," they say. "But He will come back some day. You will see Him come down from heaven the same way He went up." Won't that be exciting to see?

The Holy Spirit Comes

What are Jesus' friends doing? Are
they praying? Jesus is not with them
now. He has gone back to heaven. His
friends are sad that He has gone. But
they are waiting for God to show
them what to do.

Look! Do you see the little fire on each person's head? The fire isn't hurting Jesus' friends. What is this?

Jesus' friends know what is happening. The Holy Spirit has come. He will help Jesus' friends do many good things. He will help us do many good things too. Let's remember that.

Now Jesus' friends will tell people everywhere about Jesus. The Holy Spirit will help them do it. He will help them not be afraid. He will help us tell others about Jesus too. And He will help us to not be afraid.

An Ethiopian Hears about Jesus

Look at that chariot coming. Do you see the man in it? He is a very important man. He is from Ethiopia. Philip sees the chariot. God is sending Philip to meet this man.

Philip runs toward the chariot. Now he sees what the man is doing. He is reading from a scroll. The scroll is God's Word. Books at that time were shaped like scrolls. Philip wants to help the man know God's Word better.

"Do you know what you are reading?" Philip asks. "I need help," the man says. "Come up here and help me." So Philip gets into the chariot. He tells the man what God's Word says about Jesus. Now the man wants to accept Jesus as Savior.

So the Ethiopian leader becomes
Jesus' friend. He accepts Jesus as
Savior. Now he will tell many in
Ethiopia about Jesus. Do you think
Philip is glad he can help him? Are
you glad when you can tell friends
about Jesus?

Saul Becomes Jesus' Friend

Saul is one of the meanest men on earth. He hates Jesus' friends. He hurts some. He even kills some. He does not want people to love Jesus. He does not want people to follow Jesus. Now he is going to another city to hurt Jesus' friends.

Suddenly a bright light shines. It comes down from heaven. Someone in heaven talks to Saul. "Why are you hurting Me?" the voice asks. "Stop it!"

"Who are you?" Saul asks. "I am Jesus!" the voice says. "What do you want me to do?" Saul asks Jesus. "I want you to be My helper." The men with Saul hear the voice. But they cannot see anyone.

Now Saul knows that Jesus is God's Son. Now he knows how terrible he has been to hurt Jesus' friends. He will stop hurting them. From now on he will help Jesus do His work.

Barnabas Is a Good Friend

Saul's old friends hate him now. He has become Jesus' helper. His old friends hate Jesus. So they also hate Jesus' helpers. Saul's old friends are angry at him. They want to hurt him. They want to hurt all of Jesus' helpers and friends.

Saul has no old friends now. But Saul has only a few new friends. Jesus' followers are afraid of him. He hurt many of them before he accepted Jesus. Has he really become Jesus' friend? They are not sure.

"I will be your friend," Barnabas tells Saul. Barnabas is brave. He takes Saul to Jesus' friends in Jerusalem. He tells them how Jesus has talked to Saul.

Now Barnabas' friends are Saul's
friends too. They know that Saul is
truly a friend of Jesus. They will help
Saul tell many others about Jesus.
Don't you think we should help others do that too?

Dorcas Is Alive Again

Dorcas loved to do things for people. She washed. She cooked. She sewed. She had kind words for people in trouble. Whenever someone needed help, Dorcas was there. Do you know anyone like Dorcas?

400

Everyone loved Dorcas. You would
love Dorcas too, wouldn't you? One
day Dorcas died. All her friends are so
sad. They wash her body. Then they
put her in an upstairs room. Don't
you think they cried when they did
that?

"Find Peter!" someone says. "He will help us feel better." Someone finds Peter. Peter hurries to Dorcas' house as fast as he can. He loves Dorcas too. He knows what a wonderful woman she was to her friends.

Peter kneels down by Dorcas' bed. He
prays. Then he quietly talks to Dorcas'
body. "Get up, Dorcas," he says.
Dorcas gets up. She is alive and well.
Don't you think her friends are the
happiest people in the world?

Singing Songs to God in Jail

Do you remember Saul? People call him Paul now. He is helping others learn about Jesus. Some people do not like this. Some hate him because Paul tells others about Jesus. That's why some bad men put Paul and his friend Silas in jail.

But Paul and Silas are singing. They are singing in that terrible jail. Would you sing if some people threw you in jail? Paul and Silas are singing about Jesus. Do you think they love Jesus? How do you know?

Suddenly God shakes the jail. The
doors fly open. Paul and Silas can run
away now. But they don't. They stay
in the jail. God has some special work
for them to do there. What do you
think it is?

The man in charge knows they could
have run away. He knows these are
good men who love Jesus. The man
wants to love Jesus and follow Him too.
"What must I do?" he asks. "Believe in
Jesus. Then you will be saved," they
answer. Have you done that?

Telling a King about Jesus

That king is Agrippa. His sister is
Bernice. People are afraid of them.
They can say, "Kill him" and the soldiers will kill a man. They can say,
"Let her go" and the soldiers will let a
woman go. The people never say
anything to make the king angry.

The king wants to talk with Paul.
What will Paul say? Will he say only
nice things? Or will he say what he
should? What would you do if you
were talking to this king?

"I wish you would become a Christian," Paul told the king. "I wish you would accept Jesus." People couldn't believe Paul was that brave. What will the king do? Will he kill Paul for saying that?

The king does not kill Paul. "I almost want to be a Christian," the king says. But he doesn't become a Christian. Almost is not good enough, is it?

Paul Is in a Shipwreck

Paul must go to Rome. He must go to the king at Rome. The king will decide if Paul must die. But Paul's ship is in trouble. You can see what a stormy sea the ship is in. Will it be wrecked? Will it sink? Will Paul and the others die?

The storm keeps blowing the waves. It keeps blowing for many days. People are afraid. They think the ship will sink. What can they do? Then one day they see land.

The ship crashes against the land.
Paul and the others swim to shore.
What do you think will happen to
them there?

God takes care of Paul and the others.
No one is hurt. Some people on land
help them. God has special things for
Paul to do. That's why He takes care
of him.

A Boy Named Timothy

Timothy's mother helped him. She read God's Word to him. She told him about God. She prayed with him. That's why Timothy loved God.

Timothy's grandmother helped him
too. She also read God's Word to him.
She told him about God. She prayed
with him. Aren't you glad for grand-
mothers and grandfathers?

Does someone help you love God's
Word? Does your mother or father?
What about an aunt or uncle? Does
your grandmother or grandfather read
God's Word to you? Who does?

You're happy when others tell you about God, aren't you? Jesus is happy too. He is glad when you love Him. He is glad also when you tell others about Him. Do you?

BIBLE DOCTRINES LEARNED
IN THE PRESCHOOLERS BIBLE

Your Preschooler will learn:

424

Jesus Is God's Son

Jesus Is a Special King

Jesus Knows All about God and Heaven

Jesus Can Do Wonderful Miracles that No One Else Can Do

Jesus Pleases God

CHARACTER VALUES LEARNED IN THE PRESCHOOLERS BIBLE

Your Preschooler will learn to be:

BRAVE

FAITHFUL

FORGIVING

FRIENDLY

GIVING

GOOD

God and Jacob promised to do good things for each other.
God has promised to do good things for us.

HELPFUL

Adam and Eve helped to care for God's world.
Jacob helped Rachel take care of her sheep.
David asked God to help. That's why he beat Goliath.
God sent Elijah to help a poor woman.
Elisha was God's helper.
Some men helped Nehemiah build walls.
Joseph and Mary helped care for Baby Jesus.
Jesus' friends helped Him do His work.
Matthew helped Jesus do His work.
Jesus asked twelve men to be His helpers.
A blind man asked Jesus for help. Jesus helped him.
Saul became Jesus' helper.
Dorcas was a good helper.
Timothy's mother helped him love God's Word.

SHARING